DEDICATION

There are women across the great expanse of this world being broken open,
crying out to be heard, to find their place and their voice.
They are facing their demons, working with their shadows and gathering
centuries of deeply ingrained feminine wisdom, gifted by ancestors, whispered
by spirits and sensed into from past lives to weave their most intensely glorious, articulate and powerful
tapestry of personal centred balance.
If you have this book in your hands, you are one of those brave, beautiful and bold women.

You are doing your work, I see you.
You are on your path, I follow you.
You are shining so bright, the world cannot miss you.
We are sisters. We are blood.
We are creatures whose delicate touch and insistence on connection and truth will turn the tide to a more
mature masculine and a balanced future.
These words dear Sister are for you, because of you and to you.

Every single word,
written to gracefully find a path to your heart,
to soothe you further into flow,
to guide you deeply into your innermost private power
and straight back home to your most honest raw and authentic Self.
I hold you.
You are Held.

Lynette

GRATITUDE

A deep bow to my husband Mark for being a brave and courageous dance partner in this life time with me
and for gifting me with two most perfect daughters, Rosi and Livvie - you both hold me
and yourselves exquisitely.

Heartfelt gratitude for sacred Cacao who showed up at exactly the right time in my life
and for leading me on the most profound inner journey.

And for my guides and inspirations this year, the men and women who held doors open, who invited me in and
brought me to the Medicine Woman I am – a reverent thank you.

To the wonderful, generous, completely open people of Bali, where this book was written, every single soul who
has gone over and above for me and my family.

Terima Kasih
A'ho
Thank you

Hold this book close to your heart.
And ask it what you need in this moment.

Books open at exactly the right places.
There are secret messages everywhere.

FOREWORD

Sisterhood.
It evades so many women in our youth, as we compete and size each other up, looking to be the prettiest girl in the room, the smartest, and strongest, the most desirable.

Yet all the while, what we are yearning for is connection with each other. The ultimate sign of maturity in a woman is her ability to love and uplift her sisters. That's where we start to awaken. We discover we were never really in competition with each other; it was simply a reflection of our insecurity and fear of our power.

When a woman starts to discover her true authority, she wants every other woman to do the same. It's contagious, this fiery surge of self-love and divine feminine embodiment. We evolve from girls, to women, to goddesses. And goddesses love to congregate, collaborate, communicate, and execute world-shifting changes.

I first met the goddess that is Lynette, author of this amazing book, plant medicine mama, ceremony guardian and champion of the divine feminine many years ago, thanks to our love of the Plants. She is part human, part celestial powerhouse, part fire angel and all kinds of feminine.

She is a walking embodiment of a woman who uplifts all other women; she holds us all in our greatness even when we cannot yet see ourselves in that light. Every word in this book is meant as a prayer to the divine feminine. Each phrase was meticulously crafted to enter a woman's heart and awaken her to truth.

Our influence lies in our ability to feel, to flow through the spectrum of experience and Ms. Allen's challenge, behind every poetic sentence, is to ask us to make it all. . .sacred. Holy. Overflowing with divinity.

Now is the time, fellow goddesses, for us to look in the mirror and bow down to the perfect being that is reflected.

Now is the time to look ourselves in the eyes and say:
I see you, beautiful angel, endlessly powerful spirit.
I see your golden shadow of potentiality, all the gifts you hide away.
I see your brokenness and vulnerable heartache, the trials and tribulations you've survived and thrived through.

I see your resilient, angelic body, and the stories she tells from the incredible journeys we have lived.
I see you, I love you, and it is a supreme honour to be all that I see.
Pachamama needs all the Earth's women to rise up and know our worth, our ability to effect change, our divine healing gifts.

But we cannot create the new systems of love, protection and equality until we see who we truly are, and thereby see ourselves in each other.
This is the book that can heal and awaken the feminine.
You are holding a spark, that when combined with the essence of your golden goddess energies, can become a fire of positive change.

Drink in each channelled prayer.
Bathe in the loving intention behind every verse.
And let the feminine in you be seen, be ignited, and above all, be Held.

Tina "Kat" Courtney
Ayahuasquera, death doula, author, protector of the divine feminine

She wrote her books, she channelled her rituals,
she sourced her visions and she drank her Cacao.
She played in her magic, she lay with her pleasure,
she spoke with her gods and that's what made her smile.

TO ALL MY SISTERS

Do your work sister, do your work.
Dive into the deepest cells of your beautiful body,
bring to the surface what needs to rise,
offer oxygen and life to that which has been in the dark.

Unearth that which has been hidden,
your magic, your fire, your naked raging truth,
draw back the curtain and allow light to breathe life back into your neurology.
Allow each word to land.

Grant permission to your highest self to bring your gifts,
hold steady your private and precious emergence,
trust that your sisters around the world, their collective consciousness are holding you, sisters you know
and sisters you don't.

Sisters from every background, every ethnic culture and corner of the world are praying and
holding a light for your path to emerge.
They focus their love and attention on their growth and yours.
You are safe to do your work, you are Held.

THE CACAO PRIESTESS

Cacao is the feminine, the priestess: she is wisdom, the womb of mother earth.
She is sacred, open and invites channels of communication between you
and the realms you cannot see but that you are intricately part of.

She is gentle yet strong, she is energy medicine, an intuition opener, she is the spirit of the heart.

She will beckon the feminine in you, she will encourage your inner strength,
she will invite balance, inner stillness and unwavering knowing.

She will hold your hand as she shows you the gem encrusted pathways that
weave through the essence of you.

She will remind you of the deepest of rivers and streams that run throughout your consciousness.

She will commune with you on the ledges of the deep canyons that time, experience and lifetimes of
knowledge have carved in your soul.

She will breathe with you as you sit on the rocks watching the glistening waters of your dreams and
thoughts go by.

You will find a sacred place inside you with Cacao, a place where your answers lay, where your wisdom
flows and the priestess in you resides.

Cacao will hold space for you while you find your Self.

1

She became acutely aware of teeny changes to her vibration,
little shifts in the direction of butterflies in her stomach,
that flew in from memories or were triggered into movement by photos or words.
Those butterflies could be gathered to walk alongside her,
to face forwards with her
if she wove her magic deep inside her body.

She became so acutely aware of those flutterings,
that she could breathe with them, change their direction on a thought,
settle them from a thousand butterflies in panic,
into a strong maternal spirit with conviction in their direction.
She could choreograph their facing forward
with an instinctual knowing that her chrysalis was not her home
but a womb to emerge from.

2

She listened as she whispered wonders into the stillness.
Finger tips to her lips, quivering, she began to notice
synchronicity, messages, sign posts.
Perfect timing, path confirming.
Visions of an emerging figure, her future self.
Beckoning her, giggling and holding out her hand.
Assuring her the path was clear.
Asking her to close her eyes, breathe and trust.
They were laying stones at her feet exactly where she needed to tread.

3

Those witching hours didn't scare her anymore.
Even though fear and worry scattered her brain
and her body hurt, her breath held tight.
She was no longer afraid to get up
to revel in that time on her own.

To go outside into the darkness to meet the sounds of the night
and let them comfort her, surround her and hold her.
The stars hung in the sky, she released into the still,
was reminded of a whole world that spun on its axis without her having to turn it,
she remembered she didn't have to do anything.

She wasn't on the wrong path, she was always walking forward,
step by step, soothing herself into the vibration of expectancy.
For everything she dreamed of was already there,
had already been manifested
and gifted so many times before.

Nothing had been too heavy or hard,
everything had arrived when she needed it.
So with smiles and relief, she held her tear stained heart
brought small hands to her lips, rested her head,
breathed in love and fell back into the dream.

4

'Release' was her word today.
To release: to let go, to untie or to lift.
To return to a previous state of uncoiled-ness.
To breathe, to allow space, to unfurl.

5

When she shook, she shook to the core.
Undoing so much good work.
Conscious and aware that her path was disintegrating into dust.
But with tenacity in her soul,
never had her determination to see more clearly been stronger.

6

When she put her hand on her heart and felt
her own physical pain,
tears were released
and walls came tumbling down.

When she put her hand on her heart and
asked 'What should I do?',
words were released
and "nothing yet" was her guidance.

7

They lit candles for all the children in their lives.
The born, the unborn, the resting in peace and the secret wishes deep in their wombs.
They were able to access them with their energy,
little hands reached out,
contact was made,
apologies, words of love and reconnection.
Love and blessings released up into source,
so much healing, focus and intention,
mending hearts and healing rifts for thousands and thousands of miles.

8

Outside cacao ceremonies drinking in bliss, wrapped in blankets.
Dawn morning air, the dew and sunrise glowing.
Love in the cup and the forest close enough to smell.
A yurt and a fire distantly burning.
Barefoot on wood, lighting candles,
breathing in the freshness of new beginnings.
Dear Cacao, soothing our path...
so much love, holy communion with Self
and the beauty of this life.

9

She knew she couldn't look at the photos of the girl she used to be,
too hard, too painful, too full of dis-ease at her naivety.
She had no idea what was to come,
no idea how she could possibly feel so hurt and isolated,
unclear and struggle to breathe.
But the woman that rose from that gap,
she has something so much more magnificent than that naïve girliness.
She became the woman, the mother, the fire and the guardian,
with everything she needed hidden in caves running through secluded caverns.
She built herself on the back of a gap she never wanted.
And even though she carried the burns and stings as reminders on her fingers,
She holds herself and her journey as sacred.

10

Her altar, her sanctuary,
her place of self-worship,
her peace and her piece of the earth.
Held with respect,
gifts, finds, stones and feathers
to remind her that light shines and that life continues.

11

She spoke to plants.
Confided in leaves.
Asked questions of petals.
'Where does my heart lay?'
and 'How do I find my future?',
'Will it come to me or do I go looking?'

And they replied.

Intelligent in their answers.
Knowing in their responses.
Clear in their messages.
'Your heart is yours always',
'Your future is made by your thoughts'
and 'Stand still in gratitude while everything finds you'.

12

As she dived into the wilderness of those plants,
their spirits spoke to her, she saw them dance and waft in fields of quiet.
Voices came to her at the perfect time, just when she needed to hear she wasn't alone.
The vibration, the spirit, the strength of that drum,
the energy of the fire that breathed and danced for her transforming soul.
She closed her eyes to the world to find her own internal medicine.

13

A determination and clarity swept through her like a raging fire,
she'd been waiting for this moment.
For the sun to come up, for the storm to pass and for the clouds to clear,
she breathed air like it was the freshest she'd ever smelled,
nothing but fizzy, grounded excitement with a sturdy stillness that
spoke loud and clear.

Focus and warmth bathed her,
trust and calm overtook each and every breath,
because she had decided how to play the game.
Her navigation of storms, mist, fear and fire was exceptional,
she was spinning her priestess, her angel,
her womanhood in perfect alignment in this moment and the next and the next.

14

What if she stopped?
What if she stood still?
What if she allowed herself to be found?

15

She listened and he played,
basking in the deliciousness of his sound.
Cacao soothing her senses,
allowing source to flow through her,
filling her up, opening her wide,
smiling so deeply,
taking pleasure in every single sense.
She was moved to the core.
He stayed with her all day.

16

Heady yet grounded.
Spinny yet centered.
Overcome with deliciousness yet completely still.
Moments like these spun her to her balance, her strongest point, her sweet spot.

17

To feel in the moment so stable
and so peaceful,
knowing truly that every single wish is only ever just around the corner,
felt like a true accomplishment.
Alignment on a different level to before,
nothing more than a feeling,
energy as proof,
invisible but detectable,
already-there,
each moment bringing it closer
and she felt so deliciously excited, this was bliss.

18

And she learnt that happiness really had to be 'in the moment'.
Delicious Cacao,
heady connection to her divinity,
the sounds of nature,
the smell of fresh sheets.
If she let those moments fill her up,
the key to a beautiful future,
she would hold.

19

To the girl she used to be:

'You didn't need to try so hard.
To be more aloof, less available, more focused on you would have
made you so much more powerful darling'.

20

Without inspiration or drive
was going about it the hard way.
So many times, she had worried and stressed,
not slept, created drama and trauma for her Self.
When all that was really needed was to drop everything,
to play, to laugh, to let go of guilt and to feel free.
Inspired action emerged when she let go.

21

It was easy.
She knew this year would be the year she found her soul.
She knew this year would the year it all made sense,
where she discovered the rivers and banks and streams that flowed through her,
the glittering damns and waterfalls inside her.
Exploring those caves, she delicately lit lanterns in corners of past hurts
where wounds had scarred over.
She meandered on tender pathways,
sprinkling magic as she walked.
This was the year she had actually felt the planets line up in support of her.
Intuition told her she was so very nearly there.
So, she kept walking.

22

Her medicine, was her words.
Her rituals, were her rites of passage.
Her blessings, were the gateways to open hearts.

23

Planets did their thing,
the world spun in perfect harmony,
all she needed to do was meet her beautiful Self.

24

She took herself home every now and then.
Travelling through space and time to that privacy, that sanctuary, that space.
Where she lay in bed, in complete peace, crystal bowls at her feet.
Ruffled white sheets spilling over, bed hair and beauty.
Cacao, invitations, questions and so much love.
Stillness, fizzy excitement, plans coming to fruition.
Co-creations, working together, synergy and value.
Starlit nights, full moons beaming energy through her windows.
The depths of the earth in full support of her.
And the planets just floating about above her,
aware of her, in awe of her.
She provided, she loved and she continued to dream herself home.

25

A smile widened on her face
one quiet weekend morning.
She had everything she needed today.
She had love and silence and nature and calm.
She had water and nourishment and peace.
Today was a good day.

26

Enough. Enough. Enough.
Enough of being tired.
Enough of feeling fear.
Enough of feeling shame.
She was done.

27

While her words whispered one thing,
her feelings whispered another.
And until they were in sync,
until her feelings matched her words,
she could never walk on purpose.
So, she asked and she checked.
'What am I feeling?',
'How would I translate those sensations?'.
To soften her now,
to find her path,
to follow her truest heart,
she allowed herself to feel.

28

It was interesting, she mused, how steady her power was,
how in flow she found herself to be,
how lightly she made her way in between the petals that lay on her alter,
how she smiled and touched the stones from her ceremony the night before.

And she noticed when her space was open to the human,
gushing in, irritated, clouded and off-balance,
how she giggled inside, carefully glided around her, softening her edges as she went,
breathing deep satisfaction in for her earth, her art and her love.

29

She didn't sparkle every day.
Some days were just...well...something to get through.
Some days she was dark and on the brink of tears.
And on those days, she just hung low.
Stayed in and tried to love her shadow.

30

And she asked herself,
'What do you want to do right now?'.
And she thought.
Stood still.
Hand on her heart.
Her breath relaxing.
A smile forming.
Excitement brewing.
What she really wanted to do was play,
So she did!

31

To be pulled to the centre of her Self,
guided straight to her core,
everything slowed,
inhalation,
exhalation,
focus,
awareness.
The physical...distant sounds flew away
and a coven of sisters lifted her straight off her feet.
Fairy dust sprinkled on her path.
Her elder blew smoke on her forehead
with so much love and compassion
she thought she would melt away
and hands lightly touched her soul to breathe her back to life.

Her need to be understood was so real,
to find connection with another,
to seek commune in the spoken word and shared visions,
felt as essential as air itself.
And to face the prospect of loss,
to face the prospect of
separation, different paths and split love,
tore to her heart and her soul.
Disrupted kinship and her dreams desire,
raw wounds bled and salt dripped on them.
Stings and bites and cuts dove deep,
she didn't know how to stem the flow of grief.
So, each day she would tend to her cuts and her wounds,
sending them unending love from her source,
understanding deeply that the connection she really craved was right there.
She allowed tears to flow when they were needed
and made space for faith to flow in streams that trickled through her veins.
For now, that was probably enough.

33

You are healing, you are grounding,
you are healing, you are connected.
You are beautiful, you are beautiful,
you are beautiful and you are loved.
You have sisters, you have sisters,
You have sisters and you are held.

A chant from 'A Woman's Blessing Sacred Cacao retreat' in Bali,
from the Volcanic Sand Healing Ceremony

34

As her years passed and her wisdom dawned,
she had a renewed respect for the Self.
She recognised her value to the earth, the world and the people in it.
They played with her and she played with them,
her sense of a deeper connection to the spiritual grew.

As moons circled around her,
a strong awareness of why she was here on earth
began a new language of appreciation and love within her.
Focusing on higher states of being and consciousness,
communing with her Self, a witness to all of her emotions.

Feeling the waves, the alignment and pull of grandmother moon,
holding a higher code of conduct for the people close to her in her life,
she drew the lines of boundaries in sand dust,
as downloads came as deep as the lines on her face,
she knew.

She knew the Self, she knew Sisterhood,
she knew the essence of an emotional bond between two women
and the rite of passage to become a respectful teacher.
She made no apology for herself or her presence.
No more would she linger in the shadows, her wisdom called for a higher vibration.

35

She took herself off, she had to let it out.
The pain, the crushing sinking sad that slinked across her belly,
she folded in half onto her knees,
allowed the cries to fall out of her
and her tears to splash on the earth.

Clutching her heart, heart wrenching sobs erupted,
deep guttural sounds of pain and disappointment, she let it all out.
To a passer-by she would have looked weakened, defeated, overcome, but inside her
strength grew with every sob. For in the letting go, she refuelled and then sobs
turned to smiles and tears of pain turned into a river of relief.

Oh her heart, how it lifted
and as salty stains dissolved with cacao,
stability and stillness and deep inner solidity returned.
She was the strongest, clearest version of herself
that had ever walked the planet in this life time.

36

When she needed solitude,
when she needed cleansing,
the beauty of those canyons took her breath away.
The rockpools sang to her as she peered into them.
She could breathe fully there,
releasing everything that was too heavy.
Relief holding her hand as she sat on those rocks
and she was forever grateful for that sacred place.

37

With her hands deep down in the sand,
she dug her clarity out.
Years of comparison, lack, working out what others were thinking, in that
moment, made no sense any more.
That spilt second, she decided and she counted.
Where were they all now anyway?
Right now. Nowhere close. Nowhere near.
They didn't even care.
And that sand, the thought of her mortality; a gift.
She grew taller and made herself known.
By her own name, she would move now.
By her own name, she would be known.

38

When fear and doubt dropped in, holding hands with terror and pain,
she hadn't realised they weren't her friends until she felt their grip on her throat.
For they came in silence, without her knowing,
shadows...she'd already made them comfortable, before they took off their masks revealing
themselves as the insidious dark beings they were.

And her mind raced around, did everything it could to push them away
but the harder her mind used thought and argument and memories and worry,
the deeper they clung to her chest.
So she stopped everything right there.
Felt their weight on her lungs, felt her breath dissolve and her throat close further.

And turned those terrors into sensations,

for sensations she noticed,

were nothing more than clumps of energy that the mind entangled in story.

And as the sensations were identified,

she shone light right into their core,

allowed them to disappear, turn to clouds and dust and she laughed.

S

he cried, her tears came, sensations shifted and evaporated in her energy field.

No struggle, no fight, no fear, no blame

- just movement and clouds and energy and sunlight.

She freed herself, took deep breaths and blessed her energy field with

love and appreciation and the sincerest of adoration.

She was kind to her Self, she was blessed.

And she gave thanks
for the wisdom, the strength of age, the independence of it all.
She gave thanks for the time alone, the time in sisterhood,
the time with her lover, in love and in lust.

She gave thanks for the meditations
and the adoration and the Cacao and the union.
For the love and the conversations, for the gracefulness of her path,
for the gifts that led her here, to the essence of her Self.

She gave thanks for the reverence of ceremony
and the breath of life and of sharing and partnership and music and fun.
She gave thanks for the feminine power that led her to find home.
She gave thanks for the ease and pace of slow Sundays.

She gave thanks for his arms, his sense and his touch.
She gave great thanks for every single cell in her body that aligned
and regenerated and oozed clarity with those she loved dearly.
She loved and thanked it all, knowing it was all in her future.

40

Sister circles, sharing, plant medicine.
Vulnerability and openness on a different level.
Tears, years of grief pouring out,
stress released,
new beginnings manifested.
Touched and held by sisters who knew.
Who knew she was changed,
who saw her past differently
and who saw she had shaped a vision for her future.
And that validation,
the validation of her change,
was worth the weight of a thousand women dancing in the palm of her beautiful hands.

41

To dance around the edges of darkness, she mused,
was like trying to balance on the rim of a black hole.
A balancing act. No one ever wants to fall in.
Yet there they are; dancing and twirling and tempting gravity.
Wasting energy, flailing and giddy with drama,
peering over the edge to wonder just how far down it goes.

She knew that all that was really needed
was gentleness and calm,
poise and realignment when she wobbled.
She felt so deeply into her bones, her heart, her being,
that it was entirely possible to enjoy life on the rim,
and to welcome the breeze, the rain and the storms.

For when each one passed and it always did,
she got better and better at depending on her Self.
Her stillness and grace.
Her core so solid
even when the gods shook every cell in her physical body.
Her centre was always honoured and assured.

42

To the moon she made a promise,
whispering every word,
feeling her way into alignment, the moon knew.
With her circle of sisters,
she felt the pull of their wild,
they howled at midnight, drumming and
chanting in honour, stomping on Pachamama
'Dear Grandmother Moon
We love you, we trust you,
A'hooooooo!'

43

And when she let everything settle,
she knew she could never have done it differently.
Her younger self, all those decisions, turns, conversations, moves, all that
courage and fire and doing it anyway.
It was all practice.
Child's play for her Crone.
The foundation on which she stood, solid ground.

Tall trees grow so high
reaching through the clouds where it's always glorious sunshine and they
bask right there
soaking up the storm and rain and hail,
using the water for fuel, cleansing energy and growth.
This was who she was.
When she let everything settle.

44

She dripped into her secret self.
Creatively hiding in vine covered cafes.
Quiet, tired, introvert
and soothing her soul with Cacao, journaling and art.
A passion for words, pictures,
images and film.
Excavating deep chasms and unearthing crystals,
gems and unknown pathways inside her, was how she liked to spend her time.
Exploring places of extreme,
tumultuous pleasure,
visiting the future,
calling in her sanctuary, her heart, her home.

45

The serenity of connection to the witches, the shamans, the priestesses and the crones.
The wise women, she noticed, were falling back on themselves.
Embodying sacred eldership,
great movement meant her age was becoming her grace
and her grace was becoming her.
The power of a woman settled into her Self.

46

She lay on the floor of her own temple,
imagining the ceremony happening around her.
The singing bowls,
the touch,
the breath.
And she did her work.
Realigned her energy.
It was her greatest gift,
that she was responsible for shapeshifting her entire universe and she took great
pleasure in mining her own jewels.

Asking to bleed,
laying, holding herself
and fully exposed,
tuning into her power.
Turning gut wrenching pain and
stakes through her lungs into glorious,
woman medicine from the depths of
her womb, simply asking to bleed.

48

Imagination was her friend.
Bridging the gap between reality and her future,
for she knew that reality was actually the past.
And her future,
just a vibration to match up with.
Already there for her to move into,
she played with thoughts and feelings
and heady loved-up swirly scenarios.
Images of goodness and fun and effortless flow,
she basked in the pleasure of the here and now,
appreciating every single thing on her path
as though it was a gift from the heavens,
which of course it was.

49

Rivers ran deep through her,
each hidden fissure owned its own tiny star.
When those stars burst and filled her sky,
it was hard to breathe, black holes sucked her in.
Forced to surrender, her grip on reality ripped away.

And after many cycles, as the wind dried the tears on her cheeks,
stillness was found, at the other end of her solar system.
Stillness, clarity and new found wisdom, the secret gatekeepers smiled upon her.
Priestesses from the past gathered at her feet and she was blessed,
washed anew and gently kissed.

Moons and planets and wishes emerged,
she ran the whole damn universe through her fingers like sand, with ease,
with fire, with fairy dust.
She was her own wild, untamed medicine.
And she was the only one she needed.

50

She learned that if she didn't take great care over her thoughts,
that her secrets and private feelings would overflow into the public domain,
without her permission.
She realised the repercussions of exposing her most private self,
could be earth shattering for her.
The wounds that she had taken so much time tending to,
soothing and cleansing, could so easily
be unpacked leaving her feeling violated,
exposed and so terribly upset.
She learned she needed to be much more careful
to seek permission from her higher Self and her internal valleys in future.
To seek permission to unearth and bring to light
the whispers of her soul for others to see in full view of daylight.
For her work was internal, her work was hers and her work was private.

51

And she heard somewhere that decisions don't need to be made.
Decisions arrive.
Out of the blue.
Moments of clarity.
Some things click into place.
Planets shift.
Stars explode.
And all of a sudden, there is absolutely no way a decision cannot be made.
So. She stopped worrying about when decisions had to be made
and rather felt into the trueness of now.
Trusting that if she wasn't sure,
then the decision was not ready and neither was she.

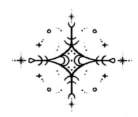

Her body, her heart and her soul, they ran so delicately deep.
No-one could ever have known of the gemstone lined pathways
that weaved through the essence of her.
No-one would ever be able to feel the diamond covered walls
with their fingertips as she did with hers.
No-one else was privy to her view
from the ledges of the deep canyons that ran through her soul.
She would sit with her feet dangling over the edge,
watching the bluest of waters trickling past deep down in those valleys.
Crystal clear. Clarity ran freely there.
Clear waters, thoughts, dreams, flow.
No-one else could float in those rivers.
No-one else could meander gently into and out
of her streams of consciousness as she did.
Glistening water held as sacred in rockpools,
she'd splash about in those thoughts and dreams,
hidden from view of everyone else.
Moon lit caverns, star lit caves running through her spirit.
They were hers and hers alone.

53

It wasn't so much her words she watched these days,
for she had learned long ago that words were spells.
But it was the energy she carried in her blood that needed attention.
For she knew that she manifested from there.
She spoke to the universe from there.
And her feelings were always answered.
Whether she wanted them to be or not.

54

The more she honoured her sacredness,
the more she grew into her Self.

The more she connected with her feminine,
the more messages her womb whispered to her.

The more her curves sang to her,
the more her touch called her.

Deeply connected. All of her.
Cells, blood, breath, heartbeat.

Her sensuality, her need and her wisdom.
Moving in sync to fill her with life, fresh energy, vital chi.

And as she stretched and stroked and arched under her own direction,
she inspired other women to move with theirs.

For when women see themselves as the sacred portals of life they are,
the feminine will rise in all of her wild, unashamed beauty, bliss and freedom will be theirs.

55

And she wrote and she wrote and she wrote,
a thank you letter to the universe,
she thanked it for every single image in her mind.
For every single intricate part of her future,
as she called it in, vibration by vibration.
She thanked it for love and passion,
for sacred circles and candles,
for medicine songs and tipi's,
for fire ceremonies and drumming,
for feathers and sage,
for chanting and medicine
and she spent the rest of the day in bliss.

56

Vulnerable, open and trusting,
she took her feet off the ground.
Carried by a thousand stars, swirling winds
and planetary forces,
they unchained her wings,
threw her shackles to the ground,
and freed her.
Only her breath to steady her,
Her silence to hold her
and her stillness to guide her.
She was on her way.

57

She realised that to step into her future,
she had to let go of her past.
Let go of the stories that held her at a lower frequency,
slowly releasing the number of times she remembered them or spoke of the drama.

To focus only on where she was going,
to align herself to the energy she was calling in.
And, while appreciating every single step on her unfolding path,
she promised to feel the excitement of the future that awaited her.

58

She saw naked feet walking on soil.
She saw a long white dress trailing past her ankles.
With her drum in her hand, she was voicing her song.
Ivy and vine spilling from her third eye
reaching for the stars and the moon.
A headdress of nature.
A priestess aware of nothing but her own spinning power.
Security under her feet.
A temple for her drum.
She let the fire burn away her fear.

Guided to a place of peace.
To steady the Goddess, allowing thoughts to sink to the floor of her mind.
Filling her lungs with fresh, clean energy,
allowing herself to just be guided to a place of peace.

60

She watched those torrential waters raging beneath her, in awe at her power.
Her emotions, her tears, her sweat and her thirst.
Her quencher, her release, her dive.
Her fight for air as they pushed her over and rolled her around in unending floods.
And yet they were also her cleanse, her pure, her safe place.
Her comfort, her calm, her rest.
Her flow or her resistance.
Her air or her drown.
Her trust or her fear.
Both her greatest pleasure and yet her greatest challenge.

61

She watched herself from a distance.
Felt her tension rise, her tone was off.
Uncomfortable. What even was that feeling?
And then right there she knew.
Shame. Embarrassment. Wanting to hide.
Relief ran through her.
'I'm learning. I'm allowed. I'm doing this.
And I'm not walking away from my Self!'

62

It had not been overnight, the process of deconstruction.
It had happened when she was sleeping.
When she'd been deep with Madre,
she'd have told you nothing much happened in those distant nights.
The shift way too ethereal for her human to comprehend.
And yet she saw it in the moments of clarity,
the moments of shedding a skin,
disguised as 'decluttering', 'throwing away', packing lighter.
There had once been a wish for to her to fill herself with earth.
And then when she did, it all became clear.
The journey, the path, the miles covered, the re-molding.
Her construction, her boundaries, her path.
Embodiment in her future, everything ahead of her, born anew.

63

When she cried her whole body shook.
When she cried, she let out lifetimes of sadness all at once.
Great waves, deep sobs, her mortal surrendered.
Flood gates opened before she could even speak.

But she spoke and he listened.
He heard her through covered eyes and rivers of tears.
He sat next to her, held her with nothing more than focus and love.
While she spoke to herself and heard her own voice.

Magical space.
Exhausted tears.
Released energy.
Calm seas washed over her and then she held her own.

64

And when the tears came and the emotions rushed forward,
she was held by her sisters,
cleansed by smoke, released, healed in sacred space.

Candles flickered,
tears fell,
breaths exhaled to catch her.

The altar, the flowers, the cacao, the stones,
bringing her back to the only thing that really mattered.
Connection to her Self.

65

She never gave up.
Even though some days were like trudging through mud.
She knew her life had meaning.
She knew she was here for a reason.
She knew she had to keep walking.
One foot, in front of the other.

66

She focused on just one thing.
Every single day,
that lifted her heart, made her smile or even laugh out loud.

And even with a head full of mist and a heart full of cloud,
the sun broke through
and opened up a whole new world.

She travelled the world with that philosophy.
Always available when she needed it.
Nothing dramatic. Just one good thing at a time.

67

She was so small.
She had absolutely nothing.
And she was sent away.
No coping skills, her whole world
going from colour to black and white.
No joy. No warmth. Just loneliness and fear.
Rejection. Rejected. Nowhere to go.
And she carried that still.
Until she brought it into the light.
And cried for that little girl.
And felt for the others who didn't know better.
And she tried to relax and soften.

And know that she grew up.
Resourceful and caped in love,
Her angels, light workers, ancestors, higher Self.
They had always been with her.
Even when she had felt her loneliest,
Deep breaths, the smell of copal, sage, frankincense.
Visions of being blessed with smoke filled her heart.
A circle of women, medicine women,
drying her eyes and deep water soothing and cleansing her.
Another part healed.
Another sore soothed.
And more, she knew, would surface.
And that's what made her wise.

68

She chose carefully.
The dress. The one that spoke to her.
The one she shone in.
The one she lit up in.

Anchoring the light.
Celebrating, with focus and intent, with care and with love.
The dress: a symbol of self-adoration,
not for the dress, or about the dress but all about her.

A self-honouring. A ritual. Ceremonial space.
Time to take herself to the altar.
Time to make promises.
Time to acknowledge her arrival.

At this point in time, she was her most precious,
her most beautiful, her most articulate and
the most valued being in the universe.
This was all for her. Everything was for her.

69

There were times when she could see straight into the future
with such certainty
that she could hear, taste, sense and smell everything
and she basked in the deliciousness of it all.

Time would pass,
she knew it would,
in her soul, everything she loved and everything she didn't,
she knew it was transitory.

And she became calmer, more in tune with the now.
The past behind her,
the future being created with every thought and feeling she had and the
present was guiding her to her centre.

70

To know.
To DEEPLY know that happiness was a place inside of her...
well, that was quite profound.
To understand it in such a way,
as to learn how to cultivate an inner environment,
to extract it from the corners of her mind and heart
when fear and worry were so very close, she could smell them.

That was a skill.
Centeredness, peace, a place of no resistance,
somewhere always there,
as she leaned into those feelings of flow and peace,
of everything working out.
Searching on purpose for play,
she realised - it had always been there, she had just turned her head.

71

To bleed was to know she was a woman.
To bleed was to know she was strong and she was Divine.

72

She knew if she waited just a little, everything
would fall into place. Sometimes time does that.
Time and the movement of the planets, the
alignment of the stars,
her asking of source
and her releasing of control.
Time, somehow, just works everything out.

Everybody had their 'thing', she mused.
Their black hole, their phobia,
their weak link, their stumbling block.
No-one, ever, was immune from that.
It was life's path.
In her strength, another woman dived into her darkness.
In her ease, another woman worked through her shame.
In doing her work to mend her own weak links,
portals of energy opened for others to mend theirs too.
THIS was sisterhood,
holding our hands out,
being prepared to catch
and also to be caught.

74

She recognised she was part of two beings.
Her human, who worried and stressed and got caught up
in fear-based indoctrination and her spirit,
who felt blessed by the energy of the sun
and trusted in the shadows of the moon.
She knew, if she let her human run wild,
she could squash everything and dampen her crazy, wild, star-spun potential.
So. She communed with her gods, her spirits, her divine.
And she asked for support and for love
and that her human be shown the light.

75

Her fear and worry took over her smile.
Concern showed up rather than love.
Distance filled the gap that connection could have.
But to those who loved her, she never went anywhere.

76

When she tumbled and crashed,
thoughts driving her crazy,
energy and motivation slashed,
it hit her.
Her mood completely relied on the actions of others.
Their bad day ran her over,
their missed promise crushed her hopes,
their unkind words slashed her dreams
and yet she knew it was her process.
To remember that her value never depended on another's validation,
her value was not reflected in their bad behaviour
and that she could reign and shine and feel the weight of her crown,
any time she damn well pleased.

To see goodness in her.
To feel compassion for her.
To know that she is learning.
To trust that she doesn't have to know everything.
To understand that life is a journey into the Self,
held her self-worth in place.

78

Living and learning,
at her heart she knew her Self.
She knew the woman she was.
Sure of every step
and resilient in the swirling of everything else.
Her gifts unfurled on every corner,
life lessons, coincidences,
random meetings all perfectly laid out.
When she hummed, she hummed the best tune ever
and people heard it for miles.

79

And sometimes. Everything. Just. Stops.
Nothing moves.
She noticed that the whole world simply froze.
The doldrums. Nothing doing. Nothing going.
And that the hardest part of that, she deduced, was the silence.

80

No smoke without fire.
No flame without a spark.
No hurricane without wind.
No passion without a first look.
She learned to navigate the elements,
the fire, the wind, the spark and the earth.
Her passion, her flame, her energy and her touch.
It was all hers.
And she was playing with it perfectly.

81

On her best days, she danced on the crystal path laid out for her.
Barefoot, feeling the cool of the precious stones beneath her,
every step a blessing.
Sparkling, breath-taking colours,
she soaked up the sensations, looking down at her earth.
Never looking ahead or behind, just focusing on the joy of now.
For the joy of now was both the future and the past in one instant.
And when they thought she wasn't looking,
fairies and spirits leapt over her toes,
and elders followed in delight on her heels.
Fairies, dream weavers and knowing souls giggled
playing in between her steps.
The magic of the unseen glistened like sparkles from the sun
and these they were her most precious of days.

82

And she knew to keep walking.
But sometimes she had no idea where she was walking to.
A destination that seemed a lifetime away.
A place to rest, so far.
Walking anyway.
Every stride, something new.
A new vibration, new scenery, a new view.
Learning all the time.
She always walked forward.
It was the only way to go.
She had no intention of turning round.

83

She gathered all the parts of her.
From all the random places she had scattered her precious Self.
Gently placing them ceremonially in her heart.
Her place of calm, rivers of gold painted over the cracks.
Breathing on purpose, bringing all of her parts together, gathering her power.

This life taught her to walk her own path.
This life taught her to hold her own space.
This life taught her to hold a relationship between her and only her.
Trust, inner strength, resilience, guidance,
nothing else actually mattered.

The pain inside wasn't lifting.
And no-one could take it away.
She had to lead her Self by the hand.
To a place where she could grow.
She just didn't know where that was yet.

86

She was trying to pull herself out of a hole.
She really was.
But it was just really hard.

Long weekends, lay ins, cotton sheets and slow kisses.
Bed hair, smiles, love and the smell of beauty.
She surrounded herself with pleasure
and tastes and deep breaths and soothing thoughts.
Opening, intention,
soft words let gently out for the universe to hear.
She trusted in her guidance.

88

She had to be awake for her soul.
She had to be wide awake and clear.
Clear about her patterns, her thoughts, her habits.
She had to be more in tune with her Self than ever before.

89

In her wild moments of beauty and peace,
she rolled around in the pleasure
of the mountains she'd moved and the miles she'd crossed.

And she recognised her youth still,
SO many more crevices to leap across, caverns to discover and creaks to jump over.
And actually, she lit up at that!

90

To stay is to sit with the pain.
To stay is to squirm in the difficult conversations.
To stay is to cry and talk and cry more.
To stay is to resist the urge to run with everything you have.
To stay is to move beyond.
To stay is an opportunity to grow deeper and stronger.
To stay is to deepen understanding, unbind old wounds and clean deep cuts.
To stay is to be present in someone else's confusion and try not to mix it with your own.
To stay is to remember why it was in the very beginning.
And to stay is to nourish, to pull close and to breathe together.

She took care to hold that space,
singing into it, spelling into it,
cleansing it with her presence, with smoke and with light.

She took care of the spirits and those who visited with curiosity,
ensuring that stillness and calm were respected,
holding medicine space, allowing the plants to do their work.

92

Her pursuit was selfish.
It had to be.
Clawing for her own truth.
And following only that.
Passionate, articulate and thirsty, a torch bearer to light the path.
Cloaked.
Witness to her own inspiration.
She walked straight into the night.

93

She felt the energy of that silent moon.
She knew a big shift was coming.
She knew she'd need every shred of trust.
And that flow would gently find her hand.
She sank into those dark mornings.
Eyes closed, barely-there breath.
And trusted and trusted and trusted.

94

Every moment became a moment to find appreciation.
To find a smell she liked, or a taste she wanted, a touch she craved.
She noticed she would smile from deep within,
linger a little longer in the bath, inhaling warmth.
Finding pleasure wrapped in white sheets, closed eyes over cacao.
Melting her heart.
Disintegrating resistance.
Releasing into softness.

95

When silence was held.
Words spilled over.
Appreciation, discovery, new lands, deep revelations.
Healing of the heart, sisterhood and sacred circle.
Sharing in deep reverence, steeped in honour and love.
THIS is sister circle.
THIS is what it means to be a woman.
THIS is our sacred power.
Gather the women.

96

Sacred timing.
If she allowed it,
she knew that everything,
absolutely everything,
was happening for a reason.
A reason far greater than her own human mind could conceive.
No idea, vision or image could do it justice,
sitting in expectation, without getting all swirled up.
Focusing on the next good thought.
In her own little world,
while her stars were forming out of sight.

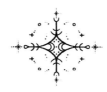

Finding new words,
to articulate, understand and be understood.
Inviting in sacred eldership,
wisdom and journeying.
Sharing medicine and finding her own.
Woman Medicine.
Medicine Woman.
Visionary. Sage and Crone.

Everything was held within a sacred temple.
Strength and tenacity and throw-your-head-back laughter.
The veil between the human and the divine.
Thinner with each decade as she learned.
She was the one.
She was the angel.
She held the knowledge.
She was the key holder, the gate keeper and the holy priestess.
And when the mist of youth lifted, she knew all along.
She had been the seer.
Sacred eldership.
Crone Wisdom.
Everything was held within her sacred temple.

99

Bathed in softness,
winds kissing bare shoulders,
far away chatters,
strumming close by.

Sunshine streaming through
cracks in clouds to remind her,
there is a plan,
you're on the path.

This oath you took,
to come into this life,
was never meant to consume you,
but to encourage you to play.

With joy,
with curious laughter
and to remember,
this is just a dream.

100

After four decades,
the cycles were appearing.
Seasons, the lunar phases, nature.
Sparkly stars and glistening seas,
they'd ebb and low,
allowing maturity, death and rebirth. That cycle.
Carving well-trodden pathways, foundations for smaller feet.
Softly does it, no earthquakes or tsunamis, just unapologetic rhythm, trust and just low.
It was all a ritual.
In her shoulders, her exhale, her body, her moon, cycles were starting to appear.

101

She had him in her head.
And she held him in her heart.
He infused every thought, sense and feeling.
He swirled her and infused every cell.
Took her off her feet and floored every heartbeat.
Yet she had no real idea of gravity, of the path or the meaning.
Just a sense and just a held breath of not knowing.

The spirit of Cacao swooned around her.
A mist of deepened gravity,
sensations of floating and being lifted.
While earths force was pulling her down,
simultaneously, she was being suspended.
And the angels came to visit.

103

She had no idea why immersing herself in water felt so good,
she just knew that it did.

She had no idea why when she felt sick to her stomach,
that falling to her knees on the ground made her feel safe.

She had no idea why her hands rose to her face when she cried,
she just knew that they did and they comforted her.

She had no idea why holding her heart when she was in pain helped her feel,
she just knew that it did.

104

She had made a thousand promises to her Self and had never kept any of them,
she had spoken of dreams and wishes and ideas and fantasies
and so many of them had never seen the light.

Yet she savoured the ones that had.
She whirled and twirled in delight recounting the joys of the visions that had broken the earth,
she filled up with the idea of possibility.

And always knew that her life was blessed,
she would always have a gift,
she would always be the gift.

105

She never gave up.
She never stopped dreaming.
She allowed ideas to flow and smiles to wistfully play with her.
She did always somehow sense that everything was working out for her.

106

As the twists of life twisted,
she began to notice that everything happened around her,
she was central and she was the player.

She was the creator, the architect, the dreamer.
The weaver, the priestess and the wand bearer.
She spoke and it evolved, she wondered and it arrived.

And she began to cool and calm and surrender.
When she felt the flames of anger lick her,
the stings of tears burn her and the sickness of the angst.

They were all so terribly insignificant really,
when she had everything already
and she was seeing that more clearly every day.

107

The stillness of a pond,
somewhere unknown,
far, far away from everything she knew.
To behold such wild elegance,
to see her reflection there,
to be so small and stare up at giant mountains.

And still be consciously aware of her tension created utter confusion.
She shook to call in stillness,
cried out in pain asking for spirits to surround her.
Drummed to the elements,
and sat on the bare earth
allowing her Self to be taken over by their spells.

Sounds disappeared from her awareness,
time slowed down
and together they found something resembling silence.
Lifted. Weightless. Held.
She was okay.
She was really okay.

108

She asked her heart
"Are you ok?"
"What do you need?",
and her heart spoke.

Words tumbled from her mouth.
Answers came. And they were not what she expected.
She knew to trust them anyway.
Because her beautiful magical heart knew everything.

109

Waves hit her and threw her off her feet.
As soon as she thought she had stability, crashing, crushing
waterfalls were tipped over her,
almost drowning her into submission.
And she always got back up.

Her connection to source never in question,
she recovered her Self,
grew to her full height*
and stared at herself in the mirror.
She knew who she was.

*phrase from Kasia Gwilliams book 'Archetype Medicine'

Warrior spirit medicine.
The truth of who she was.
Angels gliding into her body,
energy, thought and powerful attention.

Warrior spirit medicine.
To stand in her power as an independent.
As a force of nature, to stand tall and proud.
Filling herself up with love and withstanding wind and rain and earthquakes.

Warrior spirit medicine.
To breath deep and go inside,
searching for her soul, her purpose,
bringing her closer.

Warrior spirit medicine.
Healing her pains and wounds,
she heard everyone had an inner warrior
and she wondered what hers was.

Warrior spirit medicine.
She made a commitment to lean in.
To hear her whispers and see the real truth and to speak more of that.
Her warrior spirit medicine.

111

She gave flowers to her Self.
Decorated her scars and hurts.
Kissed them with sandy fingers and ocean washed shores.
Declaring her heart to the earth
and soaking her soul in a rush of love.

112

Stripped naked.
Standing bare.
Skinny dipping in the waters of life.
She was right there.
She wasn't afraid.
And she could do anything.

113

Such stillness in the morning after the night before.
Like the blue skies and the sun were completely unaware of her awakening.
The release witnessed by the moon and the stars,
in full view of them, the panic and the sobs all gone.

And the rising sun had come to clear away her remaining pain,
the energy of the night before - if she let it,
would pierce that cloud and drench her with warmth,
allowing in exactly what she wanted.

114

Making small ripples,
entering the minds of her sisters,
in distance lands,
faces and beauty she would never meet.
Words creating small moments of reflection,
relief and recognition allowing well-earned tears to fall,
holding space for moments of heartache,
celebration and self-love to find oxygen to be released.
That was her medicine
and she was bringing it to the world.

115

When she couldn't tell anyone else,
when she had words to whisper,
when she needed to put a voice to her hurt,
with tear stained cheeks and her hand on her heart,
the moon listened.

116

The moment she declared her position,
the moment she spoke her intention,
from her root, her gut, through determined clear eyes,
the universe shifted to greet her.

Her intention - a pivotal point
and never in her history had she been so fierce
to be free, unshackled without guilt or shame or ties.
Just absolutely run-by-herself free.

117

With Cacao flowing through her body,
the sun fell on her deliciousness,
as if to bless her personally,
to honour her holy sacredness.

To hold space for her and hold her gaze for that most
sacred and powerful opening.
And as she held, she rose, ever deepening, wider
circles of rippling waves and dizzy joy.

Overflow, taking her to her core,
shaking and shaken,
taken and breathless and full
with Cacao flowing through her body.

118

When she was attuned to her frequency,
she knew when she needed to sit.
Fuzzy, wavy lines, awkwardness zigged through her,
straightening it was her priority.
Tuning into her higher Self.
Sitting. Breathing. A clearer line of light to Source.
Noticing every other channel confusing her connection as she stilled.
Breath. Cacao. Intention.
Feeling her way back into the stream.
Flooding with energy, fizzing, vibrational Source language.
Plugged back in.
Swimmy, floaty, relief.

119

Grounding medicine, soothing, nurturing.
Teacher, a mirror to her soul.
A dose of truth, the reality that she'll use as a bouncing off place.
Allowing spirit to enter her quiet,
the beautiful revelations that lead her to wholeness revealed.

120

And they loved her,
surrounded her in sacred circle,
anointed her with Cacao,
wrapped her up in sisterhood
and honoured her journey.

They witnessed her growth,
standing right there on the altar,
with flowers at her feet
and Cacao on her third eye,
her heart wide open.

Words of raw and real had been spilled,
tears of the past had been released,
this was her rite of passage,
her time to flow into her wholeness,
she had been blessed.

121

To place herself on purpose,
in surroundings she loved,
filled her heart ready to burst!

To drink and taste every sip,
to sit and watch the world go by,
called her to fall into the earth.

To hear nature and feel the breeze,
oh my word...the decadence,
she didn't come here for anything less.

122

To dance with music so loud,
that each cell had no choice but to throb to a new vibration,
head shaking, rhythm pumping,
entering to get lost,
all thought slipping away,
making space for emotion to rise,
cocooning her Self in fire.
She burned and burned and burned.

Her cure. Her medicine. Her fix.

123

And she sat in blessed circle,
drinking cacao,
drenching cells and soothing,
welcoming guidance.
Finding balance,
surrounded by sisters,
protecting and holding,
expressing and feeling.
Tears trickling,
stamping feet to chanting and drumming,
shaking and releasing like witches of by gone ages.
Seeing through closed eyes,
veils and skirts lifting,
sisterhood and medicine,
circles and sage,
she remembered everything there.
A Woman's Blessing.

Quiet time sometimes pulled her in so deep,
no choice but to withdraw,
spirit asking her
to physically be still,
to breathe so she can be seen,
being called to the feet of the priestess and the goddess,
to commune, to receive their energy as hers.
Resistance was simply painful.

125

Bathed in light,
she sensed the energy in every room she entered.
Placing her hand on every single heart,
she heard every word
and spoke a language everyone understood

126

Holding anxiety, awkwardness and worry was easy.
She'd grown with it in her muscle tissue.
Well walked paths through layers of lives,
decaying, away from prying eyes.

Cool waters of communication, empathy and reading between their lines pooled on top and only when she
could hold no more, would the damn break, exposing electric lay lines.
Crippling pain striking and pounding every beautiful cell,
spasms cornering her into cold walls and chains.

'This time', she heard, 'you are inviting this',
shining lights into ancient sacred cells,
breaking patterns of feeling responsible for another's pain,
fracturing the glass house of the fixer.

She was not their answer,
merely a torch bearer for her own truth.
When it shone at her feet, others were guided
and that was the work of spirit.

127

She allowed the hands she made to hold hers.
And kiss her back to love.

128

'Listen,' she heard, 'just observe'.
All clenching released so she could see
what was actually unfolding, away from the stories.
She laughed more than she should,
all blind folds and rose-tinted glasses put aside,
her higher Self holding the picture now
and with her blessing, she saw straight through the clouds.

129

An ancient soul.
A priestess, a gatekeeper, a lover, mother, abuéla.
Tribal, indigenous, white and a woman of colour.
She held the DNA of every single reincarnation
through lifetimes of love, ritual and ceremony.
She'd felt her dreads, she'd walked in magic on distant soils
and she'd held her head so high.
And calling back her wings,
the vibrational wild that held her in a sphere of illusion,
protected and wise, walking with grace, that beautiful ancient being.

130

She missed him.
And she couldn't even tell him.
So she thought it.
And remembered his beautiful smile.

131

She was called to lay all her armour down.
To lay in peace, to give up her fight,
her attachment, her anger, her argument.
The justification, the analysis, the constant negative chat.
The exhaustion, she was told, would guide her to peace.
Surrender, she knew, would guide her to flow.

132

She called in visions of yurts and rugs and altars and circles,
of medicine, starry nights, deep journeys and drums.
She daydreamed of temples and candles and rituals with fire,
of forest edges and Pachamama and time communing with trees.

She invoked the singing and the healing, the giggles and the joy, conversations
with friends, opportunities and collaborations acting as sign posts
and runways of flight for this fairy spirit.
Each golden step she trod, another gift was waiting.

133

She became the medicine.
She was the ceremony.
Guided by spirit.
Her path lit by galaxies and shooting stars,
walking among tiny flowers,
moss covered stones and cool water streams.
Pouring sacred elixir, anointing her sisters and fuelled by gold,
her crown of nettles and feathers and ferns
kept her eyes and her focus in front.

134

Creative and thoughtful,
in sync and relaxed,
she loved the days when nothing happened.
Where arms tangled in unmade beds
and legs draped over each other,
and where those she loved, loved her back.

135

'Lay down' she said.
'Rest' she said.
'It's ok to release'.
'No need to hold on so tight'.
And she cried herself to sleep.

136

To enter her with power,
is only powerful
when she feels her own power.
She has to rise into her sovereign power.
She has to know how to handle her own sensitivity
in order to place herself as the queen.
Then and only then, can she invite the king.

137

She was there.
She didn't need asking.
She flew in with the wings of angels.
To be there, to hold and to bring her sacredness.
Generations of healers stood with her.
Her spirits and guides surrounding a circle of women.
Knowing where to place her highest self.
She was there.

138

Finding her own rhythm was a priority.
She knew that her blood was too thick and her heart couldn't breathe,
she needed to leave.
To follow the call of her own voice,
to feel the relief in every tense bone, muscle and cranial pathway,
to invite ease and release.
And it was so instant,
so soothing,
to find her own rhythm once more.

139

She learned with every curve, with every steep hill
and with every deep river crossing in which she almost drowned,
that the landscape was being created just for her.

140

When she didn't have much to hold on to,
she held on to what she had.
And for those moments,
it seemed the most grounding thing in the world to do.

CEREMONY PRAYERS

And she spoke and she shared
and she taught her secret powers
to women across the miles
who asked for her guidance.

And together they danced this dance,
with the spirit of cacao,

being guided in ceremony,
until they too wrote their own words.

They too spilled onto pages,
they too spoke words that hit sore and aching hearts,
they too held others with their breath.
She held them until they learned to dance in front of their own fires.

OPENING PRAYER

by Sallie Warman-Watts, visionary, sage, crone

We call to our Ancestors and Forefathers of this land.
Bring forth your wisdom, knowledge and love to this sacred circle.
We ask for your protection and guidance as we sit together in peace and harmony.
We open our hearts and give thanks to the Mayans and Aztecs who kept the secrets of our sacred cacao,
these secrets have long been passed down through the generations and we honour you.

We drink for all those who are lost, that they may find their way home
and for our sisters who are chained in sorrow, we drink to release you.

For the sacred Canor flower gifted from Spirit, for all, we drink for you.

A'ho

This circle is now open

OPENING PRAYER

by Tricia Allen, cacao ceremonialist

I would like to thank Cacao Spirit
and invite her energy and wisdom into this sacred space today.
I give thanks to the Mayan Gods, sending love and gratitude to the Mayan and Aztec ancestors,
who understood and cultivated this deep connection to Cacao spirit.

I send love and respect to Cacao spirit,
who is forever available to us
and guides us into our heart centre
so we can cultivate love and truly understand the spiritual energy of our hearts.

Cacao spirit we thank you for your love and guidance.
We honour all those who are drinking cacao all around the world.
To those drinking for the first time, may you be blessed.
For those more advanced drinkers, may you continue to drink.

This circle is now open.

OPENING PRAYER

by Agneta Jonsson, cacao carrier & mandala queen

In this sacred moment of serenity, stillness and peace
We allow our minds to let go of all stress, tension and flickering thoughts residing within.
We open our hearts to receive the blessings of the spirit of cacao and her beautiful sacred medicine

We invite and welcome to the circle the spirits of the directions;
East, South, West and North and the elements of Air, Fire, Water and Earth.
Asking them to bring in and infuse us with their beautiful universal qualities and gifts

We welcome the presence of and the connection to the feminine principle of mother earth,
pachamama and the masculine principle of father sky, great spirit.
Asking them to merge with each other and bring to us the perfect balance of love and light.

When we gather together, we honour and feel gratitude to the ones
who walked this sacred medicine path before us.

To the Mayans and the Aztecs, to the ancestors,
the elders and the wise men and women who found and kept the secret
of connecting to the outer and inner divinities through mama cacao.

We also feel strongly in our hearts the connection
with our sisters and brothers around the globe who serve,
sit with and drink cacao keeping this ancient tradition and wisdom alive.

So let us now honour and open our hearts to the spirit of cacao and
invite her to bless us with her divine gifts for each and
everyone's most beneficial journey and highest good.

A´ho. This circle is now open.

OPENING PRAYER

by Marina Dell'Utri, cacao carrier

To the spirit of Cacao, thank you Grandma,
for this instant grounding energy, for the now that I feel,
the moment I bring you close to my heart
and the moment your aroma meets my nose.
My shoulders drop, my belly inflates big,
my heart becomes a solid sphere of gold with an open window,
allowing fresh and cooling air to come in and out.
My thoughts stop wandering and my mind rests on a puffy, peaceful cloud, moist to the point that
it's ready to discharge rain and wash all unnecessary thoughts and worries away.

My spine anchors to the ground,
rooting the whole body deep down to the core of the Earth, the Pachamama.
I see roots wrapping around her fiery core
and energy coming back up,
straight through the body, the spine, the neck
and up into a ball of white iridescent light sitting above the crown of my head.
I feel you. I feel me.
I feel us all, human beings around the world, as a whole,
sitting with you now and celebrating you.
Cacao, what the Mayans referred to as the food of the Gods, thank you!
Thank you to all ancestors, who kept the tradition and sacredness of this plant alive.

A'ho

OPENING PRAYER

by Kirsten Kimama Lapping, sacred mesa carrier & energy worker

I invite you to feel the glowing light emanating brightly within you.
For when you shine, you are a lighthouse,
you give yourself permission to shine and give your sisters a guiding light.
You create ripples of light,
a circuit of light is created.
Connecting, by being in sacred circle,
you give each other permission to shine,
connecting to the Goddess within.
I see the Goddess within you.

Blessings,
A'ho

CACAO BLESSING

by Marina Dell'Utri, cacao carrier

May this cacao be blessed as plant medicine
and remembered as the food of the Gods.
May it be healing to our bodies, minds and souls.
May it deliver to each of us exactly what we need as of now.
It is done, it is done, it is done.
Thank you, thank you, thank you.

CACAO BLESSING

by Kasia Gwilliam, medicine woman, jungian and author of Archetype Medicine

As we open this space as sacred, we ask for support and protection of our circle.

To the element of Earth, to the direction of North and the season of Winter.
For the deep caves, for our roots and foundation,
we welcome you.

To the element of Air, to the direction of East and the season of Spring.
For our breath, for our beliefs, thoughts and communication,
we welcome you.

To the element of Fire, to the direction of South and the season of Summer.
For our spirits, for our passion, actions and potential,
we welcome you.

To the element of Water, to the direction of West and the season of Autumn.
For our blood, for our healing, intuition and emotions,
we welcome you.

To our animal and spirit guides, our helpful ancestors.
We welcome you and thank you for your presence, support and protection,
we ask for your assistance as we do our work here today.

To the Goddess Ixcacao, for your beauty, love and compassion,
we honour you and your medicine,
as we do our work here today.

To all our relations, Aho Mitakuye Oyasin The circle is now open

A MAIDENS UNICORN PRAYER

by Bex Lapping (Wakanda Phoenix), medicine woman, mesa carrier, scientist and artist

I thank the Unicorns for blessing my beautiful Cacao with divine love.

I thank the Unicorns for blessing my Cacao with their purity and bringing home my sacred inner child, allowing me to receive this world through the eyes of my inner child with bliss, joy and curiosity.

I thank the Unicorns for my divine Maiden energy and allowing her to feel safe to express her juicy self in this world.

I thank the Unicorns for blessing my Cacao with ancient knowledge, ancient wisdom and ancient magic.

My heart is open to the magic of Cacao, my heart is open to the magic of the Unicorns, my heart is open to the divine.

I promise to honour these energies, I promise to honour myself and treat these energies as the Sacred they are.

I am open to receive these energies so I may give these energies to myself, to other and to the collective consciousness.

May sacred magic walk this earth again.

A'ho

CLOSING PRAYER

by Sallie Warman-Watts, visionary, sage, crone

As we sit in wonder, thought and gratitude in this circle.
A new level of understanding begins to unfold, our hearts and our minds are now open.
To our Elders, our Spirits, our Wise ones and Angels who came to us with their knowledge and wisdom
and whispered things of the past, present and things yet to come, we thank you.

For the love and insights brought forward this day, we thank you.

A'ho – Namaste – Namaskaram – Amen

This circle is now closed.

"In the ocean waves below, is somewhere I'd like to go"
Rhoda Mai Withers

PRAISE

In deepest gratitude
for those who found these words

This book is 'the' perfect companion for any woman walking through her menopause transformation as she awakens, lets go and steps into the Goddess she came here to be.
Pages of inspiration and enlightenment what better travel companion could you wish for?

I for one shall be sharing this book with all my Menopause Rockstars.
Thank you for all you do and coming in to my life with divine timing.

Mairi 'menopause rockstar" Taylor

Every Rising Woman needs to read this book.
It delicately resonates to the very core of the children we once were.
It's as though Lynette has travelled through my mind and articulated my thoughts, feelings, sadness, and hope.
Closing my eyes and wiping my tears after reading Held,
I can picture myself passing this on to the child I once was,
as her right of passage to womanhood.
A beautiful poetic medicine for the soul.

Elle Angeline, reiki healer

Lynette Allen is a profound Medicine Woman,
she gives instinctively with her new book, all women, without exception,
'Permission' (we think we need) to walk our own path in the absence of prejudices and in reverent honour.
Insightful, intuitive and deeply spiritual.
This book is a blessing.

Sallie Warman-Watts, visionary, sage, crone

Lynette has done it again - wow!
This book feels it is her story wrote for all of us, it is my story, it is Lynette's story, it is your story.

Lynette is pure unicorn magic with her delicious words, awakening cells and memories,
allowing the sisterhood to rise and the Earth keepers to be again.

Lynette's medicine is so needed in this time and here to help heal the collective sisterhood wounding.
Together we will rise as one.

I felt so alive reading Lynette's book and in fact did feel 'Held' by her words knowing the darkness and
demons I faced (and still face) were all for a purpose, to allow the light back in.

It gives us permission to be our juicy self in this world and arrive just as we are, perfectly imperfect.

Tears flooded from my eyes as I felt a sigh of relief reading this book,
we no longer need to be at war with ourselves, we need to feel all of our juicy parts in order to heal,
we are safe to do this.

Hope ran through me as I read these powerful intoxicating words showing me that I'm safe,
I'm ok, I'm held.

Keep rising women, keep reaching out, keep reading Lynette's books we no longer need to hide sisters,
we no longer need to be repressed, we are here, the divine feminine is here alive in this juicy book and she's
planning on staying.

Bex Lapping "Wakanda Phoenix" medicine woman, mesa carrier, scientist and artist

The best gift I bought for my daughters was a mooncup each,
so they could release shame, bless the earth and be proud to bleed and be women.
Now I can give them something better.
'Held' is a powerful book of women's wisdom,
so my daughters will now know that they are part of an intricate line of
powerful women who are doing the same.

Skie Hummingbird, plant medicine woman, mother & mystic

Within seconds of reading Lynette's words I felt tingles,
like my soul was speaking and receiving all at once.
Her words had spoken once again.
My soul tingled knowing it would once again receive insight, wisdom
and I would be held once more by this wise woman's words.
The title of this book speaks volumes for how it will connect,
I hear you, my soul hears you and I am so looking forward to sharing this in our Sacred circles.

Thank you, thank you.
A'ho beautiful soul

Kirsten Lapping "Kimama", energy worker and sacred medicine carrier

Thank you, thank you, thank you!
Another absolute dream of a book for women everywhere.
After sharing 'A Woman's Blessing' in my work with women over the last year,

I have seen lives changing before my very eyes!

I am absolutely thrilled to share 'Held' with my Tribe.
Another gem for Women.
Blessings to you Lynette for all that you are, and all you do.
With so much love and gratitude.

Andrea Jackson, women's spiritual guide, mentor, cacao ceremony & circle holder, elemental yoga trainer

'Held' is a sacred collection of words that heal women.
As I read through this beautiful collection of verses,
I was in awe at the soothing flow and depth of meaning.

This book will be set on my alter next to Lynette's last book, 'A Woman's Blessing'.

If a woman is looking for an Oracle, this is at the top of my list.

Lynette is a gifted writer, channeller and healer.
Thank you Lynette for cultivating your gifts through the written word.

Lynette Marie Allen, intuitive astrologer, medicine woman and wise seer
(no blood relation to the author Lynette Allen but soul sisters never-the-less)

This book felt familiar, like an old friend returning to share stories, to reminisce about old times, to laugh and to hold me in arms full of love, understanding and feminine grace.
The words shared here, while compiled from the wisdom of Lynette's heart,
speak to an experience we all share.

The experience I speak of is femininity, sisterhood, of being deliciously and unapologetically woman.

While we all have our own experiences of what this means to us,
Lynette captures the heart, the truth, the pleasure, the questions,
the struggle, the pain, the grief and the sacredness of our collective experience.
Each passage contained exactly what I needed in the moment,
that I, in my curiosity, allowed myself to be chosen to receive its wisdom.

Laughter, recognition, solemn realisation;
the gravity of each of these passages should never be underestimated.
I found myself on every page and continued to unravel the mystery of what it means to be connected to
the feminine as I drank in her words.

This book is one for your altar, for your circles, to reach for in times of need,
times of love, times of crisis and times when another sister calls for your support.
'Held' provides continual nourishment, archetypal familiarity, unification, community and the knowing
that wherever you are, you're not alone.

No - you are Held, sister.

Kasia Gwilliam, medicine woman, jungian and author of Archetype Medicine

I am a Mother, a Sister, a Midwife.
I am also so much more.
I am a Woman who is discovering her own authenticity, unable to recognise who she used to be,
yet recognising herself on every page in this book.
A beautiful collaboration of poetry for the awakening soul.
Her words had the safe effect. Beautiful.

Lisa Harris, midwife

First off...wow!
Honoured to have read these words,
like a cool crystal clear spring in intention, beautiful.

I dived in and didn't want to emerge.

Lynette's words relay a journey all women/sisters know in their hearts.
Exploring what it means to be 'Held' and exploding stars of enlightenment as you read.

Together with 'A Woman's Blessing' these powerful books offer the gift to dig deep within ones own cave.
With insights and wisdom into sisterhood and self practice,
Lynette's spirit allows us to truly dance in her words.

Jo Sellars, earth mother, energy healer, red tent & nurture circle holder

Beautiful reminders to allow yourself to feel,
of how to truly hold space for yourself,
to know that you are the medicine and that you are never alone.
Guidance of how to release the harsh pressures we often re-create again and again.

Words that nurtured me me back into balance with my nature.

Kirsty Kaye

Lynette Allen's soulful, purposeful prose will resonate with women everywhere.
This book is a soothing balm for those of us whose expertise is in holding and not yet in being held.

Lynette gives gentle voice to our deepest desires for sovereignty and sacred Self.
Her wisdom guides us as we begin to breathe again and take the barefoot steps back to ourselves.

Xanthe Eloise, instinctive meditation & transformational change coach

Lynette takes you on a journey through the scripts of her heart.
Her sacred rising is a graceful dance with the divine.
Wrapped in silky stars howling under the moon, she walks into her sovereignty.

Vanessa Shari, sound meditation practitioner, ceremonialist & medicine woman

A TRILOGY

'A Woman's Blessing - Nourishment for the rise of the feminine'
was the first written in this trilogy.
'HELD - Guidance for the rise of the feminine' is the second and
'Sacred - Integration for the rise of the feminine' is the third.
This is the journey, a woman's journey, it's your journey.
May it nourish you, guide you and support you in your cohesive and beautiful rising.
Blessings on your journey dear sisters.
May you know you are always Held.

GATHER THE WOMEN

Gather the Women is a 22 day immersion into the 3 aspects of ourselves,
the girls we used to be, the women we are now and the women we are yet to become.

Women across the world from Australia, US, UK, Europe and Asia,
have joined these small (mainly on-line) sister circles.

22 days of cacao ceremonies, ritual, blessings, meditations and rites of passage.
This is not to be undertaken lightly, it's a journey into your Self,
with a small committed group of women all doing their inner work too.

Expect tears, expect laughter, expect to listen to another's story, expect to have your heart
touched, expect drop-the-mic moments, expect gushings of love for yourself and every
other woman there.
Expect peace, expect acceptance and expect to be changed.

Lynette has trained other women to hold their own gatherings also,
so message @gatherthewomensistercircles on instagram for dates of all their gatherings.

GATHER THE WOMEN
- Part 2

And then there's Gather the Women 2...integration and elevation, this is next level.

Advancing your relationship with the woman you are yet to become,
you'll playfully dance with the girl you used to be, listening to the wisdom she offers
and embedding your commitment to honouring the woman you are now.

Plus we introduce our 4th aspect, our higher selves, making a connection to the stream of consciousness
we all have access to but so easily forget, mistrust or block. This is the channel where the women we
are yet to become speak to us from and this is the channel we will clear, learn to feel the flow in and find
our own ways of receiving and sensing clarity beyond just words.

GATHER THE WOMEN FACILITATOR TRAINING IS ALSO AVAILABLE
To be eligible to become a Gather the Women facilitator,
you must first have gone through Gather the Women 1 first.

ABOUT THE AUTHOR

A daughter, a mother, a wife and a grandmother.
She is gentle and wise, a woman of medicine
and she finds her words carefully.
Tears spill as effortlessly as her spells,
her heart is open to break as visibly as it is to blossom (which it does often).
A king and two daughters hold space for her to spin.
Ceremonies and rituals keep her on an earthly plane,
while spirits call her attention.
Learning to speak to, with and through them, trances overcome her.

Eyes closed.
She speaks words,
translating messages through silent energy.

Her fires and drums move her,
her song and words moves them all.

A secret holder
with a private heart,
she weaves her way.
Always.

STAY CLOSE

Celebrate your own feminine power and show us how these words impact your own
spells, rituals and ceremonies with photographs, flowers & cacao.
Join us on Instagram

@thelynetteallen
@awomansblessing
@gatherthewomensistercircle

and send your appreciation to our medicine sister, tattooist and illustrator @ami_suel

Made in United States
North Haven, CT
12 June 2023

37650810R00107